Let's Look Under The City

What's going on down in that manhole under the city streets?

Nobody lives under the city, but lots of important things are going on down there out of sight and out of the way.

Did you ever wonder how water gets to your faucet or electricity to your lights?

This book will let you look under a city and see how it is all hooked up under the ground with pipes and wires for water, electricity, gas, telephone, and waste. After you read the book, the next time you see an open manhole, you will have a pretty good idea of what's going on.

By The Same Authors

HOW BIG IS BIG

LET'S FIND OUT

LET'S LOOK INSIDE YOUR HOUSE

NOW TRY THIS

YOU AMONG THE STARS

HOW YOUR BODY WORKS

ROCKS, RIVERS, & THE CHANGING EARTH

MORE POWER TO YOU

Let's Look
UNDER THE CITY

By Herman & Nina Schneider

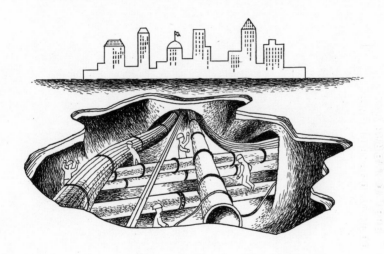

Illustrated By Bill Ballantine

NEW YORK: WILLIAM R. SCOTT, INC., PUBLISHER

Library of Congress Catalog Card No. 54-6791

COPYRIGHT MCMLIV AND MCML BY HERMAN SCHNEIDER. MADE IN U.S.A.

Contents

APARTMENTS FOR RENT 7

WATER ON TAP 9

DOWN THE DRAIN 23

SNAP A SWITCH 33

COOKING WITH GAS 45

THE LINE IS BUSY 57

NO VACANCIES 69

Apartments For Rent

Up goes a new apartment house, high up in the air. Day after day, workmen bang and hammer. Day after day, people stop and look and listen.

Up go the steel beams, higher and higher. Up go the brick walls, higher and higher.

When will the new building be ready? When can the families move in with their children and canaries and carpets?

Will the building be ready when the walls are finished? Can people move in when the roof and the floors are done? No, not yet.

Floors, walls, and a roof are not enough. What else do people need before they can move in?

7

Water On Tap

People need water. You can't bathe a baby, or rinse a quince, or spray a spaniel without water.

You can't boil the beans or soak the socks without water. Water washes shirts and dishes and dirty necks. A cool drink of water is fine when you are hot and thirsty.

Water, water, water! Everybody needs water for so many things!

How will the people in this new building get the water they need?

When the building is finished, people will turn on a faucet and out will come all the water they want.

Now, all through the building, plumbers are busy. They are connecting tubs and sinks and toilets and wash basins to water pipes in the wall. These pipes run from the top floor down to the cellar.

When the plumbers are finished, every faucet in the building will be joined to a water pipe. Every sink, every tub, everything that uses water will be joined to the pipes that come from the cellar.

But pipes are not enough. We need water in the pipes. Where does the water come from?

Let's look under the city and see.

Water for the new building will come from a big pipe called a *water main*. The water main is under the street.

A workman is joining a pipe from the building to the water main. When he is finished, water can flow from the water main up into every water pipe in the building.

There are water mains under every street in the city. They are buried down in the ground under the street where they are out of the way and where the water won't freeze even in very cold weather.

Every house and office, every store and factory, reaches down under the city to the water main.

Every faucet and fountain and hydrant gets its water from the water main.

But where does the water in the water main come from? Let's look under the city again.

If you could follow the huge underground pipe that brings water to the city, you would come to a big lake. This lake is called a *reservoir*. Water for the city is stored in the reservoir.

After it leaves the reservoir, the water is sent through a building called a *purifying plant*. Here it is cleaned of any bits of sand or dirt or germs.

Then the water is sprayed up through fountains, so that air and sunlight can make it fresh-smelling and clean-tasting.

The fresh, clean water flows down into the big pipe that brings it to the city.

But where does the water in the reservoir come from?

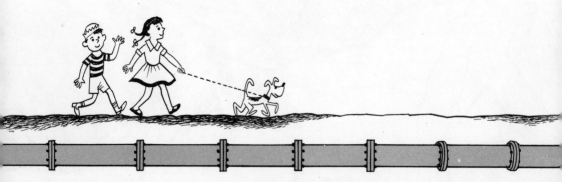

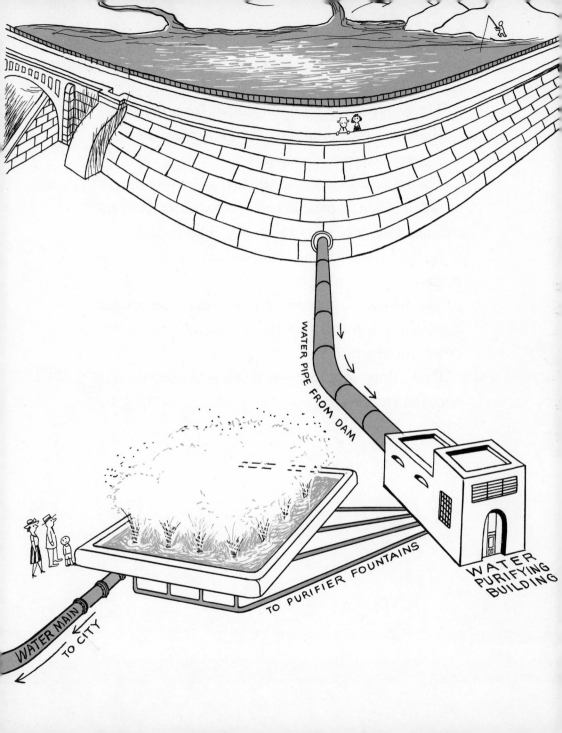

WATER PIPE FROM DAM

WATER PURIFYING BUILDING

TO PURIFIER FOUNTAINS

WATER MAIN

TO CITY

The water in the reservoir comes from the sky.

High over the mountains, far away from the reservoir, rain falls from the clouds.

The rain soaks into the spongy soil of the mountainsides. Then, when there is more water than the soil can hold, it begins to seep out, little by little.

It trickles and bubbles into mountain springs and brooks.

The brooks flow down into streams. The streams come down together into rivers. And the rivers flow down into the reservoir.

Every drop of water you drink is a raindrop that once fell from the sky.

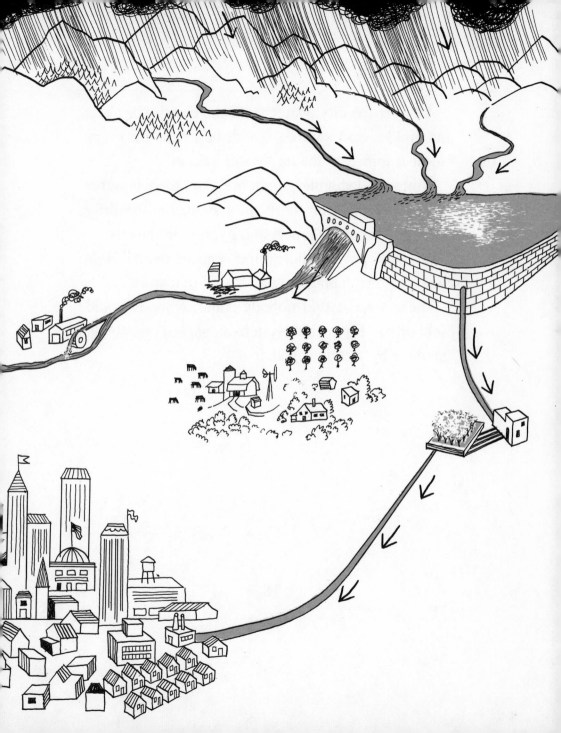

All over the city, water from the clouds sprinkles and tinkles and swishes the dishes, because every faucet is joined to the city water system.

Winter and summer, night and day, there is water for the laundry, for the beauty shop, for the drug store, and for every faucet and hydrant in the city.

But who put all those pipes underground? How could anyone manage to pay for all that work?

The answer is that nobody could. Nobody could build or pay for a water system alone, but everybody can do it by getting together.

People have found that, if they work together, they can get clean water by building a water system. It is easier this way than for each person to dig his own well or carry his own water from rivers and ponds.

It takes many people to get a water system going. Engineers are needed to plan it. Other men dig ditches and lay the water mains, build the dam and the purifying plant.

Then, after the water system is built, other people are needed to keep it in good working order.

And each time a new building goes up, it, too, is joined to the city water system.

Down The Drain

Now the building will have all the water it needs. Now it is joined to the water system, like all the other buildings in the city.

Now there is water to bathe the baby, to scrub the puppy, to wash the dishes.

But when the dishes are done, and the baby is washed, and the puppy is scrubbed, there will be lots of dirty water.

You can't just toss dirty water out of the window. Where does all the dirty water go?

The people in the new building won't have to toss dirty water out of the window.

They can thank the plumbers for that, because the plumbers are busy putting in dozens of little drain pipes, called *waste pipes*.

Before they are finished, every sink, every shower, every toilet, every basin will have a little waste pipe connected to the big waste pipe in the wall.

This waste pipe goes down to the cellar, too. But it doesn't just empty the waste water on the cellar floor.

Let's see where the waste water goes.

WASTE PIPE

← TO SEWER PIPE

The waste pipe from the building goes out under the street just like the water pipe.

But are the plumbers connecting this waste pipe to the water main?

Of course not! You wouldn't want your supper cooked in dirty water, would you?

The waste pipe connects with an entirely different pipe under the street. This big city waste pipe is called a *sewer*.

The city has miles and miles of sewers to take away all the waste water from homes and factories, from schools and offices, from stores and garages.

Rain water, and water from melting snow, pours into the sewers, too, from gutters in the streets and from the rooftops of houses.

But after the waste water pours into the sewer, where does it go?

In many cities, the waste water flows along through the sewer, out of the city, until it reaches a place called the *Sewage Treatment Plant*.

Here the waste water is pumped and sprayed through tanks and machines that take out the waste material. Sometimes this waste is hauled away to be used as fertilizer.

Then the water that is left is pumped out into a nearby river.

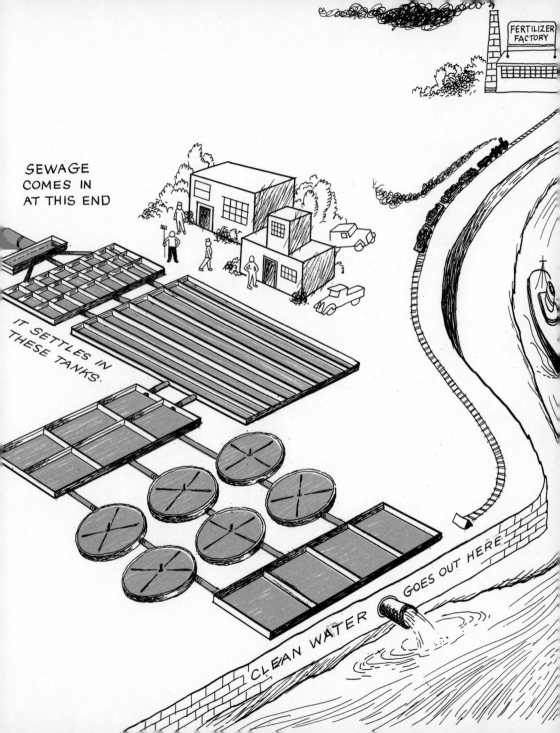

But there is waste that can't go down the drain—chicken bones, tin cans, wilted flowers, broken toys, worn-out shoes.

The people in the building will want to get rid of these, too. And they will want to keep their street clean.

Getting rid of all the city's waste is a big job—too big for each person to do by himself, as he did in the olden days.

Instead, the city has a clean-up department.

The clean-up department buys sprinkling trucks, and trash baskets, and sweeping equipment, and sewer pipes. It hires engineers and street cleaners.

And everybody pays his share of the cost of keeping the city clean.

Snap A Switch

Now the building has water that comes in and water that runs out.

But another thing that people will want in their homes is electricity.

They will need electricity for light at night. They need it for their beaters and their heaters, for their radios and their vacuum cleaners, for their electric clocks, their refrigerators, their television sets.

Shut your eyes and see if you can remember all the sockets and switches in your house.

The new building will have hundreds of sockets and switches.

How does electricity get to all those places?

From every switch, and socket, and electric outlet in the new building a wire runs back through the walls out of sight.

These hidden wires are all connected to long, long wires that run down inside the walls to the cellar.

When the electricians are finished putting in these wires, electricity can travel through them to every room and hallway in the building.

But where do the electric wires get their electricity?

Is there electricity under the city, too? Let's look again and see.

Yes. There is electricity under the city, too.

Down at the bottom of a manhole under the street there is another electrician working.

He is joining the electric wires from the new building to one of the big electric cables under the street.

But where does the electricity in the big cables come from?

If you could follow the big cables that bring electricity to the city, you would finally come to a house, called a *power house,* where electricity is made.

The Power House is usually next to a big lake with a dam, like a reservoir.

Water from the lake falls down through big pipes. The falling water turns huge water wheels inside the Power House.

As the water wheels spin, they turn big machines called *generators.*

Generators make electricity.

In some cities, the generators that make electricity are turned by steam engines instead of by water wheels.

But whether a generator is turned by steam or by water power, it makes the same kind of electricity.

38

Electricity zips out of big generators in the power house.

It flows quickly through cables to every street, and then up through smaller wires to every house.

Then more wires bring the electricity to every electric outlet in every room.

All over the city electricity races through so many places—the street lights on every street, the traffic lights on the corners, the dentists' drills, washing machines, elevators, electric clocks.

Just think of all the electric signs, and movie houses, and factory machines that electricity runs all over town!

Long ago, there were no television sets, or radios, or other machines that work by electricity. There was no electricity.

People lit their homes with candles and with oil and gas lamps.

A candle or an oil lamp is a simple thing that each person can get and run for himself. But a city electric system is not.

Specially trained men are needed to plan an electric system, and build it, and keep it running.

It takes everybody joining together to build and run a complicated thing like an electric system.

Miles and miles of electric wires, sewers, and water mains under the city! It's crowded down there!

But there are still other things everybody needs that come from under the city. Can you think what they are?

Cooking With Gas

You can't cook a custard, or fry a fish, or bake a cake, or roast a roast without some kind of heat in the stove.

You can get heat from electricity or kerosene or wood, but the people in the new apartments are going to cook with gas.

Gas stoves make heat by burning gas, and the gas has to keep coming or the flame will go out.

How does the gas come and where does it come from?

Gas comes in pipes. It flows through pipes like water, even though you can't see it.

And here are the plumbers again.

This time they are putting in pipes that run from every gas stove in the building down to the cellar.

Gas will heat the hot water for the new building, too, so in the cellar, one of the gas pipes goes to the water heater.

Just like water mains, there are big gas mains that run under every street in the city.

Here, a plumber is joining the gas pipe from the new building to the gas main.

Let's follow the main and see where it starts.

If you could follow the gas main to the place where it begins, you might have a very long trip ahead of you.

Most of the gas in this country comes from gas fields. These are special places where there are great amounts of gas deep underground.

The gas comes up through holes that are drilled deep down. These holes are called *gas wells*.

The gas that comes from underground is called *natural gas*. Long pipes carry the natural gas to almost every part of this country.

In some cites another kind of gas is used. This kind is called *artificial gas*.

Artificial gas is made from coal. The coal is ground up and heated and turned into gas.

Then the artificial gas is stored in a large tank.

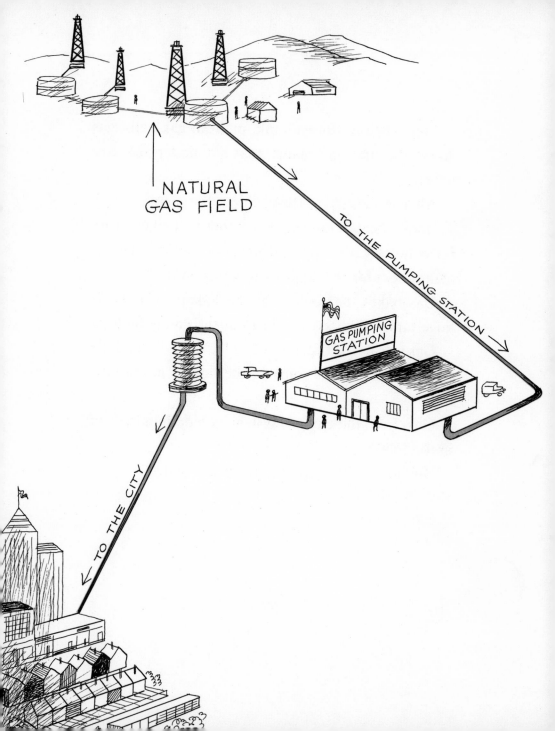

NATURAL
GAS FIELD

TO THE PUMPING STATION

GAS PUMPING
STATION

TO THE CITY

From the big storage tank, or from gas wells, gas flows into the gas mains that go under the city streets.

All over the city, gas heats things for people.

Here it heats a kitchen stove, there it makes steam for a tailor's pressing machine, in another place it makes heat for the dentist's tiny gas burner.

Gas bakes the cookies at the bakery. Gas heats huge tanks of chocolate syrup at the candy factory.

Gas warms the tiny pots of fudge sauce at the soda fountain. Gas heats some of the houses in the city, too.

Gas, from the city gas system, can do hundreds of useful jobs.

But how did the city gas system get there?

Building a gas system is a job that no person can do alone.

Lots of special machines are needed for drilling gas wells or making artificial gas.

Pipes must be laid across valleys and under rivers, and under every street in the city.

To do a big job like this, people join together in a city gas system.

Do you have a gas water heater in your house? If you do, you use three whole systems every time you take a bath.

The water system brings the water to your house. The gas system brings the gas to heat the water. The sewage system takes away the dirty water.

Miles of pipe, dozens of pumps, hundreds of engineers and thousands of other people were all needed just so that you could take a bath!

The Line Is Busy

The new building is almost ready.

The gas pipes are in place, and so are the waste pipes and water pipes and electric wires. Everything is joined to mains and cables under the city.

Only one thing is left to do.

When the families move in, they will want to talk to friends and relations and have celebrations. To do this they will need telephones.

They will want to call the movie theater to find out what's playing.

They will phone the doctor to ask what to do about the baby's sniffles.

They will call the repair man to come and fix the TV set.

Most of the families in the new building will want a telephone.

Hurry up with the telephones!

Inside the building, telephone men are busy all over the place putting in telephones.

Each telephone is joined to two wires that come out of the wall.

The wires from all the telephones go down through the walls to the cellar.

But a telephone is of no use unless it can be connected to other telephones.

How do the telephone men do that?

From every telephone in the city, two wires reach down and join the big telephone cable that runs under every street.

Right now, down in a manhole under the street, a telephone man is joining the telephone wires from the new building to this cable.

But there are many telephones and wires and cables all over the city.

When you call up a friend, how does the message that comes from your telephone find its way to your friend's telephone?

And how does his answer find its way back to yours?

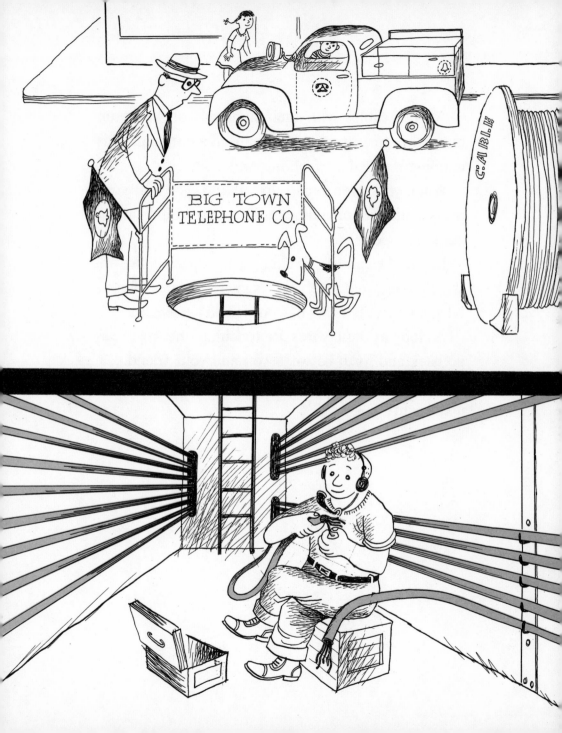

All the cables with their hundreds of wires run under the streets to a switchboard in a building. This building is called a *telephone exchange*.

When you want to call up a friend, you dial your friend's number on a dial phone, or you tell the number to an operator.

In the Telephone Exchange, an operator at the switchboard, or a machine, touches the wires of your telephone to the wires of your friend's telephone.

As long as these wires are touching, messages can go back and forth between you and your friend.

"Hello. When are you coming to see us in our new apartment?"

CABLES
UNDERGROUND

From city to city, from country to country, all over the world there are cables that connect telephone exchanges to each other.

Through these cables you can speak to a friend in another city, or in another state.

Even if your friend is in Alaska or in Africa, you can still speak to him over the telephone.

The telephone system covers almost every part of the world.

Not so long ago, if you wanted to talk to someone at a distance, you couldn't just pick up the phone and call him.

You could make smoke signals, or send a message by a friend, or telegraph, or write a letter.

But none of these ways of talking was as quick or convenient as the telephone.

Just think of what a big job it is to connect you with people all over your city, all over your country, all over the world!

Think of how many people had to work together to make that possible.

No Vacancies

Now the new building is finished. The families have moved in with their children and canaries and carpets.

Now the people can cook meals in their new homes, wash and iron, take showers, play records, invite friends, have birthday parties, light up Christmas trees, do homework at night, or listen to the baseball scores.

They can do all the busy things a busy family does because the new building is connected to the pipes and cables down under the city streets.

Now the holes in the street are covered over, and the traffic rolls along.

But under the street, out of the way of the traffic, there are water pipes and waste pipes and gas pipes, electric wires and telephone wires all ready to work for the people who have moved into their new homes.

Under the street a building keeps on going. It reaches down and it reaches out.

It becomes part of a city that reaches out to the rest of the world—to the rivers and the mountains and even to the clouds in the sky.

GROCERY

MOVING

MOVING

BATH

STREET

TELEPHONE CABLE

ELECTRIC CABLE

GAS MAIN

WATER MAIN

SEWER

ABOUT THE AUTHORS

HERMAN AND NINA SCHNEIDER are a husband and wife writing team. It is hard to say who does what, but, in any case, they have collaborated on a great many outstanding science books for children as well as a very successful series of elementary science textbooks published by D. C. Heath.

Mr. Schneider taught science for many years and was Supervisor of Elementary Science in the New York City schools. One of his great gifts is the ability to make science concepts clear and related to everyday living.

Mrs. Schneider has had experience as a teacher, librarian, editorial consultant, and editor. She is a devoted reader of poetry and approaches the facts of science with a poetic sense of wonder and delight.